Artist at Large

By David Paul DeMars

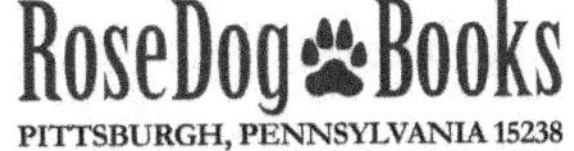

RoseDog Books
PITTSBURGH, PENNSYLVANIA 15238

RoseDog Books
585 Alpha Drive
Suite 103
Pittsburgh, PA 15238
Visit our website at www.rosedogbookstore.com

ISBN: 979-8-88683-309-6
eISBN: 979-8-88683-702-5

AMERICAN EXPRESS

I got back to the studio and checked my calendar for work. I didn't have anything booked for two weeks. I was pretty broke with nothing pending. I went through my notes and made a few calls only to find out that the next opportunity was two weeks away. I thought, What am I gonna do?

I decided to go out to the mailbox to see if the mail had arrived and found an American Express card had been sent to me, even though I hadn't filled out an application. Calling American Express and talking to an agent, I said I'd just received a new card and needed to know what the credit ceiling was on the card because I was going on vacation. He said a lot of people spend $5,000 on vacation, so I figured that was my credit limit. I wasn't aware that unlike other credit cards, you had to pay the full balance within thirty days.

I didn't want to sit around waiting for my next job, so I called a travel agent and booked two tickets to Hawaii by swiping my new American Express card. I called a girlfriend and asked if she wanted to go. We should be leaving in two days for a ten-day trip. She agreed and said she'd be ready for the trip, just pick her up.

In two days we left for the airport. I hadn't yet booked a hotel, but figured I'd just "wing it." Once we arrived after the seven-hour flight, I had her stay on the beach while I found a hotel. I found a nice room not far from the sand and swiped my American Express card for the room.

I continued to charge everything from meals, drinks, groceries, T-shirts, surfing lessons, Captain Cook's cruise tickets, scuba diving, and anything else that struck our fancy. Finally when I was buying some souvenirs, the clerk said, after she'd swiped the card, that American Express wanted to talk to me.

"Hello, David DeMars here."

"Sir, what are you doing?"

"I'm on vacation. You know, 'Don't leave home without it.' I'm using my card."

"Sir, you have no history with this company."

"Well, I'm making history now!"

"How much longer will you be in Hawaii?"

"Just a couple more days then back to work. I'll send you a check when I get back."

"Enjoy your stay, sir."

As I was skateboarding around, I ran into a woman

with a small souvenir stand. While looking at her stuff (a lot of touristy junk), I noticed a small wooden statue on the ground next to the stand. I knew from some studies that I had done in college that it was a primitive carving. it was a Papuan fertility figure from Micronesia, off the coast of Australia. I bought it for $25 and asked if she had anything else like this piece.

She then began to tell me a story about her "Indiana Jones" type husband who had gone up the Sepik River to trade with the primitive tribes for their ancestral art. He was trading T-shirts, tank tops, and sunglasses for their stuff. She said he had died about a month ago and that there was a large crate of his collections at the airport, but she couldn't pay for the storage. The company that was holding the crate was about to seize it for the bill that was due. I said I'd sure like to see it, and maybe we could work out some arrangement to save it.

We went out to the beach and after a couple mai tais, we went to the airport to see the crate. After peeling back the door on the crate, I saw that there were at least eighty pieces, some totems five feet tall, some grass skirts and masks, shields, and many small carvings—all covered in dust and cobwebs.

She offered to let me take the whole crate since she was pretty broke and didn't want to lose the crate to the storage people.

"Maybe when you get this back to the mainland, you can send me some money."

I said I could just charge the shipping ($800) on my American Express card. I got her address, paid the shipping clerk and the back storage fees, and went back to the beach to share the story with my friend. We stayed another day, then flew back to the States. We'd had a real blast!

Once home, there were many messages, and one that really made my day. A designer that I knew was doing a big nightclub down in LA that had an African theme. I called her immediately, and told her that I had a lot of primitive African-type art that she could surely use in the interior. The crate arrived and I sent her pictures of the art.

She bought about half of the collection for $9,000 and gave me the lucrative commission to do the interior painting. I put the deal together, delivered the work, and sent the woman back in Hawaii $3,000. She got back to me and said it saved her life. I then paid American Express the money owed to them. I still had $6,000, and the rest of the collection that I sold out one piece at a time over the next few years.

THE PLASTIC PRINCESS AND THE SINGER

I met the neighbor of a doctor I was working for in Palm Springs. I was introduced by the doctor's wife. The neighbor was a woman who had just undergone some serious plastic surgery on her face. She said that when I finished the doctor's work she would like me to work at her place next door.

I decorated the doctor's interior in faux-painted walls with illustrations of gothic masks in sienna color over the massive drapes in the front room. There were also several murals I painted copying Rene Magritte, a twentieth century surrealist, and a Norman Rockwell of a doctor and a child—fitting since he was a pediatrician. I created a trompe l'oeil alcove with a large bouquet of flowers in the powder bath. All went very smoothly. The kitchen walls were painted to imitate red brick and mortar. Then various country accessories were added. I finished and was paid handsomely and went next door to see about what the neighbor had in mind. Her name was Shelly.

Shelly greeted me at the door and began

describing various ideas she had and we quickly made an agreement to start the work right away.

That's when it started to get weird. As I began to paint for her, she put on some music by the singer Lou Christie, from the '60s. She said she had gone to his concert, and that she was going to divorce her husband and find a way to meet this guy and marry him…he lived in ENGLAND!

As I proceeded with the paint, she hired me to do storyboards to illustrate a play she had conceived that was based on his music. That was how she intended to meet him and marry him. Well, I did all the illustrations and she took off for ENGLAND!!

While she was gone, I was still painting various designs in her home. I got to meet her husband, an attorney, and he told me a little about what was going on as he read the paper and smoked his cigar and I painted.

I finished the work and was paid by the husband (soon to be ex) and I went on my way.

Shelly called me back some time later to say she would like to have me paint for her again at her new home, but she needed some time to get some money together because she didn't get anything in the divorce. She hadn't gotten past Christy's publicity manager with her play and dreams of a celebrity marriage.

A PLEASURE TO WORK WITH

I had been working for a couple that was into selling furniture and helping people design their interiors. We had been working together for about ten years when they decided to expand their business by establishing a showroom in which they could better sell their furniture lines.

The first showroom was approximately 10,000 square feet of concrete floors and black walls and a ceiling made of air-conditioning duct, etc. etc. etc. The cost was $14,000 dollars for paint. I received a deposit and went to work on it. The ceiling was sprayed black first then the walls were all faux-painted with various colors and designs including some small murals and Venetian plaster walls. The floors were then color stained to look like various forms of stone and marble to embrace and present the expensive furniture lines they were to sell. This whole process took about a month until the furniture was finally installed.

Now, the lady in the couple was always nice and

we had a nice relationship where I helped her with her clients that needed paint and design and she helped me by getting me the job, and receiving a nice referral sales commission. Her husband, however, was a total asshole and I wasn't the only person who felt this way about him, including his wife. He finally decided to leave the building next door and do another showroom and so he called me and asked me to do the new building and wanted me to begin work ASAP. I figured I could do this with his wife, and try to stay out of his way as much as possible.

Upon asking me to do this new project, I said that I would bring them an estimate and collect a deposit on the agreed amount, and that I could begin work in about a week as I was finishing another project. This proposal apparently made him angry and he began to shout, "What's the matter? Don't you think I'm going to pay you?"

"Well, Wayne, I'm not your employee. I have my own business and this is how I work. Do you want to agree on a deal…or what?"

"No deposit, just get here and get the work done and I'll pay you."

I replied, "I don't work that way but perhaps you could find someone else to work on your terms." Upon leaving there, he yelled, "Oh yeah, well I will… and if anyone asks me who did the work in the other showroom, I'm going to tell them you died."

What a nice guy—eh? He then hung up on me. I shrugged it off and forgot about it. A couple of weeks later he called me back and asked me if we could work something out because he tried working with a couple other artists, but it wasn't working out.

The only thing I could say was "I'd like to but I can't."

"Why not?" he asked.

I just replied, "Cause I'm dead."

THE LAWYER AND THE POSTAGE STAMP PANTIES

I got a referral from a previous client so I called and made an appointment to see what the man wanted. He was a big-time lawyer with his own firm. He greeted me at the door and asked me to come in to discuss what he wanted done in his interior.

He had everything well planned out down to the last detail called out for every room. He wanted a mural of the creation of Adam by Michelangelo on the dining room ceiling, Venetian plaster walls, faux aged walls, and a multitude of colors throughout the house. His much younger girlfriend sat at the table with us, but when she started to speak, he yelled at her to keep her mouth shut. "I only want you here on Tuesday, Thursday, and Saturday!" he exclaimed rather loudly, and I didn't hear another peep out of her. I left with the contract signed and check in hand. I was to start the following Monday.

This was a four-bedroom home and he wanted every square inch either painted, striped, or faux painted with some decorative borders as well. He said he would meet with me each morning before he went to his office to approve work, but I rarely saw him at the end of the day. He would usually leave me payment increments as I progressed. The girlfriend was usually leaving as I arrived, a bit worse for wear.

The Michelangelo ceiling was done first, with a striped wall at one end, and was approved quickly. He asked me to move on. One room after another was finished until I finally got to the master bedroom. He had selected a yellow color which seemed a bit feminine to me but that was his choice. The master was quite large with a settee at one end with lounge chairs and a desk. There was a wooden box on the desk that held his collection of Rolex watches that kept the watches on time and running. The room was finished with two coats of paint and ready to put the furniture back in place when he came in and began to feel the walls with his hand.

"I would like you to paint this again," he said. "I want a nicer feel."

"Okay, but I'll have to charge you for another coat, more paint and labor."

"Fine. Money is no issue…just paint the walls again."

I didn't paint the bedroom again by the time I saw him in the morning the next day, and hadn't put the furniture back in place, because I was working in another area. "Did you paint the walls again?" he asked as I followed him back to the master. He didn't give me a chance to answer before he began rubbing the walls with his hand again. Then he must have assumed it had been painted again because he said, "See, much better."

He then asked me to paint the inside of the walk-in closet a bright blue color. Upon looking at the inside of the closet I saw about a hundred gray suits, five electric tie racks, and about fifty boxes of shoes, most of which were new and hadn't been used. After carefully removing all the suits, shoes, and ties, the closet was painted and everything was put back in place. When he met me in the morning he asked if I had painted the inside of the built-in cabinet.

"How am I supposed to do that?"

"Take out the drawers, paint the walls in the back of the cabinet, then put the drawers back in. See? Simple. So just get it done to complete the closet. Then I want to know if you would like to paint and decorate my next house. That should happen in about five years or so."

"Yeah, okay. Give me a call when that happens."

The last thing I had to do was finish the laundry room and ceiling. I came across a basket containing six pairs of women's panties… I'm talking about a tiny piece of material with some string. I couldn't help but hold up a pair to appreciate. The girlfriend appeared at the door right then, and we met eye to eye for a moment. I finished and was leaving when she handed me her phone number. The next morning he met me and did the final walk through and gave me my final payment, saying he would call me in about five years to do his next house.

SHEILA

Went to a prearranged meeting at a home in Malibu Colony, California with a woman named Sheila who had found my website online and asked to meet about some wall art she wanted at her home. It was Monday morning.

The house was built right on the water, kind of a large cottage look. I rang the bell at the gate, which was an antique wooden door with two large Chinese Foo Dogs, one on each side. The buzzer went off and I went into the front door through the garden. The door was open so I went in and said, "Hellooo!"

After a short meeting she decided to hire me to age the walls and paint some angels in trompe-l'oeil in the dining room. We agreed on a price and I was to start right away.

I went to work on the aged walls and the angels. Other people of the trades were changing various things around the house. I didn't see her until I was finished about a week later.

When she saw the work, she loved it and said she

had another idea that she wanted me to paint. She opened a large art book and revealed what she had found. There on a three-page foldout was the Sistine Chapel Ceiling painted in the Vatican by Michelangelo hundreds of years ago. It is recognized as one of the greatest masterpieces ever painted. It took Michelangelo fourteen years to complete....

She said "Isn't this neat? I saw this and then measured the dining room ceiling and the shape isn't far off. I think it will fit." I was thinking to myself, Jesus Christ!

Then she told me that she was having a big party on Saturday and would like it finished for the party. I said, "Well, Sheila, this was painted by Michelangelo—"

"I've heard of him," she interrupted.

To which I wanted to respond, "Let's give him a call," but I didn't. Instead I assured her that I couldn't complete this by the weekend, explaining to her that there were over three hundred figures and a lot of architectural renderings, and that it would take quite a while to put this together. Her reply was "Oh, I've seen you work. Just get to it."

Well, I hate to disappoint, but...aw, come on! She asked me if I wanted the commission or not, so I said I'd get back to her on this one.

A couple weeks later, she called me again

because she had another idea. So I went back to talk about her new idea she had another large art book titled Masterpieces of the World. The whole book was ear-marked with about twenty pieces of paper slipped between the pages. She sat at the table with the book in front of her, opened it, and said, "I want you to do some copies of these paintings in oil paint." She ripped a page right out of the book. "I want this one." Then on to another page…RIP… out came another page…then another…RIP…I asked her to stop.

The three paintings were from the seventeenth century. One was a floral arrangement in an ornate vase on a table that had a beautiful cloth drape. The second was a Madonna and child and the third, a landscape with a castle. It was at this point I noticed the white powder around her nostrils, and that she looked pretty LOADED.

"How much will this cost? I want them to be large and framed in big gold frames. And how long will it take?" she asked.

These were masterpieces, but I knew I could do a great job if given the time. "Each painting will take about a month to complete, so three will take ninety days. This is an order and has to be paid in advance. They would be $5,000 each, totaling $15,000."

"That's fine. It's Phil's money anyway." Phil was her husband, who was a really nice, very wealthy man.

She whipped out the checkbook and wrote out the check. I gathered up the pages and put them back in the book.

"Well, thank you. I'll be back in touch when they are completed."

Over the next three months I worked on the paintings until I was satisfied with how they looked. Then bought the frames and was ready to present them to her.

When I called, Sheila answered, "Hello."

"Hello. This is your artist. Your paintings are ready."

"Paintings? I don't know anything about paintings." Then she hung up.

I figured I'd wait for her to come to her senses and call me back, so I put the paintings in the corner of the studio and waited for the call. I had other assignments to work on, but after about a month, I figured she wasn't going to call, so I called the house, and Phil answered. He said he didn't know anything about any paintings, but "If Sheila hired you to do something, you can just keep it. I don't want anything to do with it. She's a coke head, and I'm divorcing her. I threw her out!"

No problemo. I ended up selling them to someone else.

TWELVE SURGEONS

With good fortune, I was able to get a call to airbrush a ceiling in a surgery center in Reno, Nevada. The designer that I was working with had signed to decorate the interior and felt the ceiling was a "must."

I was to call and make arrangement to schedule as the current rate of construction was on full go and this was a ground-to-finish new building, which needed all a surgery center would require. What made this project possible was the twelve surgeons in concert as a corporation working with the city and state to make a surgery center, not a hospital. The difference between a surgery center and a hospital, is as long as the patient can finish their procedure and leave within twenty-four hours, then it's not considered a hospital, different regulations.

So I looked at the plans and the ceiling was quite large in the reception area at 35'x75'. I sent them a proposal and a cost of $8000.00, which the doctors all agreed to. One doctor called and asked how soon

I could start. I said, "As soon as you send me a check for the eight grand." …crickets…. He said he would get back to me.

About two months later he called again and wished to talk about how long it would take and would I consider a deposit of $1,500 to put this forward and when can I start. "As soon as you send me a check for the eight grand."…crickets…. He said he would get back to me.

Now you may wonder why I stayed steadfast in my negotiations. It's hard enough to please one doctor…. I'm supposed to pass the critique of twelve surgeons and everybody else.

Thirty days later he called again with another adjustment to the terms, and I told him the same as before that a check for the eight grand would be nice, and then I'll shoot up to paint a magnificent cloud ceiling. I sensed that they were running out of time and that they had gotten other artists' costs and input. And the flooring and wallpaper was to be installed very soon.

Before long, another doctor called and said the check is in the overnight mail if I can paint the ceiling ASAP. I said, "Sounds good…I'll see you at the site… after I get the check.

My bank honored the check and I flew into Reno, rented the necessary truck and scaffolding and went straightaway to the anthill of a project. A doctor approached me and said "How soon will you be done?"

I replied, "I'm going to get some breakfast and start the paint and it shouldn't take more than three days to complete." He said, "Hey, I don't get breakfast at a time like this."

"You should, Doc. It's good for your health."

"I know, smartass." He gave me a stare and was perspiring as he turned and walked away. The setup went well after draping all the walls and floor, because the wallpaper and flooring were already installed.

The painting went smooth as silk and an effect that I hadn't planned made the work look even better. The flat acrylic went over a satin, slightly shiny surface that added a little shimmer to the sunset fade at the rim of the ceiling…. The work was well accepted by all, so I cleaned up and returned the rental equipment, got on a plane and headed home, happy as a peach in a peach tree. I found out a little later that the doctors had sued the cement company that did the foundation, the general contractor, medical equipment provider, the installers, the designer and pretty much everyone…everyone except…me.

PISS ON MONEY

I got a call from an Arab guy referred by a former client. He wanted to meet with me about doing some work on his house. He gave me the address and a time to meet that would be later that day.

When I arrived at the house in the Hollywood Hills, I was surprised to be greeted by him at the door wearing full-on cowboy gear, complete with chaps and a vest. His eyes could burn holes in wood.

Once I got inside, the whole house was decorated like the Wild West… there were bull skulls, bull horns, a pair of antique chaps mounted on the wall, various spurs of different types, cowhides…you get the picture. There was a carpenter installing some fake beams in the living room and my job was to paint the walls in a rustic finish and stain and age the beams to look old…Okay…. Didn't see the owner for a couple of days, but his wife was home while I worked and she, too, could burn holes of her own in oak.

I worked with the carpenter to install and paint and age everything. When the owner appeared next he was dressed as a full-on Arab dude. He had silky garments, but what was odd to me was his arms were bound with leather straps, and he was chanting under his breath as he paced around. Then he disappeared into the back of the house. A few hours later, I was finishing when he reappeared again in full-on cowboy gear.

I told him I finished and would like to get a check for the work. I believe I mistakenly said, "money."

"Excuse me, I was wondering if I could get my money today?"

"Money, money, I piss on money. I piss on money." Pronounced "peese." I could smell burning wood, but stood up to the task.

"Well, that's all fine and good, but I'd like my check please…." More burning wood.

But alas, he sat down and wrote me the check, while muttering "money, money, I piss on money." I felt fortunate with all the "peesing" that the check was dry when he handed it to me. He disappeared into the back again and I grabbed my stuff avoiding eye contact with the burning eyes of his wife.

NO TIME FOR ROMANCE

It took me pretty much all day to get back to my place. The pad had a small apartment in the back with a gallery/studio in the front. I collected rents for the landlord, so he gave me a great deal on the rent. The apartment had a small living room with an adjacent bedroom and a small kitchen just off the living room. A bathroom was between the living space and the studio. I got home and went in the bath to turn the water on to take a shower.

When I came back out, a girl I was seeing was sitting on the couch. She hadn't called, so I was a bit surprised. I told her I was going to take a shower and would be out in a minute. About fifteen minutes later, I came out into the living room wearing a towel. To my great surprise, there were now three girls on the couch, all girls I was seeing…gulp!

I had to think fast. So I went into the kitchen and opened the fridge, grabbed a beer, and exited out the back door, jumped into the van and took off.

I drove around for about an hour in just a towel and

no shirt, so I got some looks from other motorists, and eventually ended up back at home. I figured that the girls would have all gotten mad and left, but again to my surprise, one girl had stayed… She just said "Where you been in your towel?" Sheer Luck Holmes rides again!

MRS. CHO

I hopped in the van and headed off to my next assignment working for an Asian woman named Mrs. Cho. She had a large house, complete with eight large columns, and twenty-foot-high ceilings.

She had selected her colors, bright orange and intense yellow. You practically needed sunglasses the colors were so bright. But if that's what floats her boat, so be it.

As I began the work of coloring the walls and marbleizing the columns, Mrs. Cho would constantly ask me about ten times a day, "Dabid. You use two coats, yes?" To this I would respond, "Yes, Mrs. Cho, I have to paint two coats so that the paint covers properly." Each day she would say the same thing. "Dabid. You paint two coats?"

After the fifth day of her saying the same thing over and over, I got an idea. The next time she asked, "Dabid, you paint two coats?" I responded, "Mrs. Cho, I should tell you that I'm a professional painter and artist. Experience has taught me that if I paint the second coat first, then the first coat, that will complete the paint coverage, so it looks right and finished." She looked puzzled but stopped asking about the two coats.

She decided to have me decorate the upstairs bedrooms since she was very happy with the work so far. We picked out the colors and I told her I would return in the morning to begin work on the bedrooms. She gave me a check for the new work, which I deposited and went to the paint shop and purchased the additional materials, the colors and all the faux glaze for the effect she desired.

When I got home, there was a message on the phone that said I should call Mrs. Cho right away. When I called her, she said she'd changed her mind and that she was going to do something else in the bedrooms. Upon hearing this, I told her I had already bought all the materials that we had agreed on. They were all custom colors and I couldn't return them, but I could gladly refund the rest of the deposit she had given me.

She began to scream bloody murder in Chinese. I couldn't understand a word, but she kept screaming and wouldn't stop. So I hung up the phone, knowing she would call back.

"You hang up on me, Dabid?"

I said, "You keep screaming and won't let me talk."

"I want all money back; I no pay for materials."

"But I already bought the materials and can't return them."

She began to scream again, so I hung up again. She called right back. "Dabid, you no hang up on me when I scream. I hang up on you!"

"Go ahead," I said. And she hung up. I never heard from her again.

MOM'S OUTTA TOWN

Got a call from a woman requesting that I faux paint the interior of her home, all walls in the living and dining rooms. I told her I'd be right over. Got her address and shot out the door.

It was a beautiful home on a tree lined street, well maintained with lovely gardens. Went to the front door and rang the bell. A woman answered and we hit it off very quickly. She showed me the places she wanted done and we agreed on the cost. She was going out of town for a day or two, and her husband was away, but her sons would be there to let me in. I was to start in the morning and meet with her to get the color approval before she left. As I was leaving, I noticed a set of drums in the family room with some guitars and asked her who plays. Her sons she told me. I said, "Thanks. I'll see you in the morning."

I got to the house at about 9:00 a.m. and took the meeting and got the color worked out. As she gathered her portfolios for her meetings, I set up tarps and ladders, etc. and began to work. About the time she left, two of her sons, about eighteen and nineteen years old, sent her off with a "don't worry," and a peck on the cheek. The eldest was still upstairs.

Once she'd left, after about fifteen minutes, the eldest came downstairs holding a bong in one hand and a 40 oz beer in the other. He began to chant "MOM'S OUTTA TOWN, MOM'S OUTTA TOWN!" Over and over between large drags off the pipe and large gulps from the beer bottle. The other two sons joined in and began to play the drums and play the guitar while chanting "MOM'S OUTTA TOWN." This went on as they smoked their way into Stonerville.

I just kept on painting. They invited me to join them, but I said I had to work. The house began to fill with smoke. Then a very attractive young woman came in and said she was going swimming.

I was painting by the window that overlooked the pool, when I saw her strip off her clothes and dive in. SKINNY-DIPPING TIME! She started to swim back and forth with the band playing in the background. I was kind of hoping she would do the backstroke. I wasn't making a lot of progress by the window when the front door opened and in came the mother.

"WHAT IS GOING ON HERE?" She had forgotten something. She and the eldest got into a shouting match. Apparently the girl heard this and jumped out of the pool and got her clothes on while the two were fighting. I hung by the window.

The girl came in and played the polite card like "Hello Mrs. Cleaver, what a nice home you have." The mother said she had to go, but added, "WAIT TIL YOUR FATHER GETS HOME." Out the door she went with what she had forgotten. The two other brothers had kind of disappeared for a bit, but once they heard the car leave, it was right back to…you guessed it…"MOM'S OUTTA TOWN."

Unfortunately, the girl didn't go back in the pool. So I painted past the window.

Next, a neighbor kid of about twenty came in without knocking and made himself a very large sandwich. He came over to begin to complain to me about his dad. apparently, he was supposed to do the dishes, and his claim was that he didn't get them dirty. He continued to complain as mayonnaise dripped from the side of his mouth. I said, "If I were you, I'd move out and get your own apartment, keep a steady job, and do it while you still know everything." He walked away and joined the band in bong hits.

The mother returned late the next day, and I was already finished. She was sorry about the thing with her son, but they would get that handled when her husband returned. I packed up and said thanks for the work.

BLUE MONDAY

I got a referral from a job I had done on a very large apartment complex that was decorated in a lot of marble. My job there was to help decorate the models and marbleize all the large columns (fourteen of them) that were in the foyer of the building. My new referral had leased one of the units and wanted me to paint and decorate his unit in a plum color. The walls, columns, fireplace and most of the unit was to be done in this color, so I made the deal and came back the next day to start work.

No sooner had I started, that I learned he was a pornographer. Exactly what kind, I choose not to delve into. However, different people of this endeavor were periodically stopping by to visit, sign papers, etc., but no photographs took place while I was there.

At one point, though, while I was marbleizing the two columns a young woman had reclined on his sofa and began to masturbate and make moaning sounds. I tried not to get distracted but "Really!" She soon finished what she was doing and left.

The pornographer was a fat man, maybe 300 pounds. While I was painting, he had hired a personal trainer to help him lose weight. The trainer had him take Bee's Honey Serum, Vitamin E, Vitamin B23 and all other sorts of concoctions while he pushed this man to exhaustion on a treadmill and stationary bike.

I finished the apartment and he gave me a check that turned out to be "insufficient funds." I had to have my bank collect for me as I didn't want any more involvement with this individual. I learned a couple weeks later that he died of a heart attack.

THE AWESOMES

At this point in time, I was hoping to get an art job that required a lot of skill and talent at a place where art was appreciated. The Awesomes job fell into place.

My brother, a fabulous glass artist got an assignment to install some very large glass panels on a home in Pacific Palisades and he needed some help. He picked me up and we went up to the top of Sunset Blvd. with the glass. He was telling me about some other work he was doing there as well, more artistic work, and that his client was quite wealthy and very nice. Upon arriving at the job, a complete remodel, a red-tailed hawk flew five feet away from me and landed on a branch. A good sign, I thought.

We unloaded the glass panels and carried them up to the big brownstone and set about the task of the installation. While I was helping him do this, I ventured into one of the eight bathrooms to discover an artist painting a mural on the wall. He had wallpapered the wall with canvas and it looked as if he didn't know what he was doing. I thought the painting was not very good—like it sucked—but just got some water and went back to work on the window panels.

Later I happened to notice the artist loading up his gear in frustration and disgust. He'd been fired by the architect of the remodel. The world-famous architect began ripping the canvas off the wall with great enthusiasm. I went back to work on the glass.

As I began to look around at all the workmen of various trades, and the immense size of this beautiful home, and all of the beautiful furniture and lamps and paintings, I thought, WOW, this place is awesome! On one side of the house was a view of the entire city of Los Angeles and the coastline. On the other side was a view of the beaches of Malibu in the distance beyond a giant pool surrounded by gardens. The servants' house was quite large as well, nestled back in the garden, where a family that did the cooking and housekeeping lived. The entire property was surrounded by a very elaborate wrought-iron fence that was about 1,000 feet long.

Back in the interior where everything was being changed like on a movie set, the painters were finishing the glass-like paint coat finish on all the doors, while the two designers moved and placed the new furniture and hung the artwork, which consisted of many museum-level paintings by Picasso, Chagall, Miro, Max Ernst, Paul Klee, and many others. I later got a chance to appraise the collection, using Christy's Auction House catalogues, at $250 million. "Hey, these people got coin!"

We finished the glass installation, and my brother happened to mention to the architect that his brother, meaning me, was an artist. The architect said to tell me to talk to the designers. They need an artistic painter. My brother introduced me to the designers, two gay fellows, somewhat elderly, as they passed by with a woman I mistook for another designer. Turned out she was the Madam Awesome. I got good eye contact and a smile from her, which made me feel good. She softly said, "We'll give you a chance." AWESOME! So, I got hired as the new artist on the house. Upon meeting Jon, the head designer, we immediately hit it off. We had good chemistry. He thought I was funny and vice versa. He gave me my first assignment, which was to work with Harry, the famous architect...lovely....

When I met with him, he instructed me to patina (colorize) the entire wrought-iron fence that surrounded the property. That'd be 1,000 feet of elaborately designed wrought iron. HELLO!!!.... I suggested that we make the patina from rust preventative products, but he insisted on using

Liquitex, a polymer (plastic) material (water-based) paint. This paint cost $12 for a small six-ounce jar. He then showed me a formula he had devised the night before which entailed mixing three different colors together, tediously, one at a time, so that the metal was marbleized in a bronze-like appearance. MISTAKE! However, since this was a Polish army drill, that's one general and one private, I had little choice. Remember the last artist.

After finishing the glass installation with my brother, Richard, I wrote up a proposal for the paint on the fence and Madam Awesome wrote me a check saying "Any money you need for this is fine." I put the check in the bank on the way home and picked up some materials to start the next day.

The next morning, I got the okay from the architect and went to work on the fence. I worked shoulder to shoulder with the landscapers and painters on the exterior until they finished about the same time I did, three and a half weeks later. I submitted my invoice to Mrs. Awesome and she paid without blinking and thanked me for doing a good job and for being fair on the cost. She said there were many other things that had to be done and to talk to the designers. I showed them my portfolio, and they gave me another job. During that night someone had left the garden gate open and some deer got in and ate $4,000 in flowers that had been just planted. Mrs. Awesome came out and calmly said, "I guess we'll have to replant." I suggested if that happened again, they should have a barbecue with venison.

My next assignment was to come up with a wall finish to color the walls of the master bedroom in a glaze that would work and enhance the curtains that had been hung. They were a shear goldish, silver-fish, pearl-essence feel. I started the next day after getting some coin and purchasing the right stuff. The assistant designer asked me what color I was thinking, so I said, "Master bedroom? How about BONE!"

He called me a savage. "Just match the drapes."

I had a friend be my assistant, to help drape the room and assist me in applying the glaze. I thought to do one small wall and get that approved before finishing the entire room. That way, if they hated it, I could repaint. Doing the whole room and then have them hate it would truly suck.

So, I went and asked the designers to look at the sample wall and see what they thought about it. They said they would bring Mrs. Awesome to see it. Just then, the architect came in and I asked him what he thought of the wall finish. He looked like he was ready to explode. His hair seemed to stand on end, and then he exclaimed. "This is horrible. They'll never approve this." I thought it was super. The architect stormed off. My assistant was shaking and asked what we were going to do now. "It's not up to him, it's up to Mrs. Awesome. Let's see what the designers and Mrs. Awesome think…I'm not afraid."

The designers and Mrs. Awesome showed up soon with the architect in tow. The designers asked the Mrs. what she thought…she said "I love it!" The designers followed with "Yes, very nice…. What do you think Harry?"

"I think it's terrific too," he said. Then they said to do the rest of the room and thanked me, and I gave the architect a funny look.

They, the designers, gave me another job right away. They took me to the powder bathroom near the front door that was already done up like a jewel, in glass and crystal designs throughout with gold leaf walls, with fine silver lines tracing through.

They said the only thing that didn't fit the design was the ordinary toilet. They instructed me to match the toilet color to the wall design. Interesting, no? I stated that I would have to wrap the room in plastic sheeting, cover the floor, then proceed to decorate the toilet and that I would charge $750 for the task, because I didn't want to do it. They said, "Just do it."

I got to work on it the next day after acquiring the proper materials. By the end of the day, it was finished and the match was perfect…it had to be to get approval. They checked it out and gave me the green light by saying "Spot on" and I submitted my invoice and was paid. After a couple of days, I went back to see it again, and there was a regular-looking toilet where the decorated one had been. I found one of the designers and asked what was up with that.

"Oh Mrs. Awesome thought that toilet was too loud, so we installed a quieter one for her. Repaint it the same as before to match the walls. That's another $750. I said, "Okay" and redid the paint…$1,500 for a gold-leaf toilet.

The one designer thought this was so outrageous that he took me to another bathroom and asked me to match the toilet to the leopard-skin rug—a leopard-skin toilet. I thought that was kind of crazy, but said okay and matched the toilet to the rug…another $750…. Then the other designer came in and hit the ceiling and screamed, "Whose idea was this?"… "Your associate," I said, and he stormed out. They had me clean off the enamel paint that took me almost an entire day, but they paid me for the work…Who's complaining?

As I came out to the front room a painter was touching up a wall with white paint right above a Picasso. I asked him to stop and took the painting down and set it aside until he finished and rehung the piece before anyone saw.

Next day, when I came back to work on the nursery, I had to go out to the van and get some materials. Two men in black suits and sunglasses were walking up the drive. Secret Service. I recognized who they were because I had driven a limousine for Spiro Agnew when I was eighteen. They were doing surveillance of the house because Bill Clinton was coming over to see the Awesomes about campaign financing. I couldn't help myself, saying, "No Jehovah's Witnesses please." They didn't smile.

The Awesomes were always super nice and respectful. The Mrs. had contracted a nasty cough from the dust of the remodel and couldn't seem to shake it off. I suggested a healing meditation could help. Since nothing else was working, she said she'd try it.

I suggested we walk out into the garden, which we did. And I told her after the meditation, her cough would be gone. Apparently she believed me because she asked if I would then get her cough. I said no, it doesn't work that way.

I stood in front of her and asked her to take my hands in hers and close her eyes and I would take her on an imaginary, peaceful walk through a forest near a small stream and we would end up stopping at the pool of tranquility. All done in a very calm, low voice. When we arrived at the pool, I asked her to visualize the sun in her mind and to place that image directly between her eyes and to feel its heat. This area is the ajna center. I then asked her to hold it there as long as she could. We stood silent for a few minutes. Then I told her to open her eyes and her cough would be gone. Miraculously, she stopped coughing and didn't cough after that. Auto suggestion? That's when she started calling me Super Dave.

When I was finishing the nursery, the designers and she were looking at a set of antique pottery from the eighteenth century to buy from the Design Center in Beverly Hills. They loved them, four in number, but they were a bit too expensive, even for her. But she had them delivered to the house so she could see if they worked. They were about $4,000 each for the 10-inch vases and one tureen, very beautiful all covered with sculpted flowers. She asked me to look at them, since I'd told her I was a potter. I said I could produce some copies at about $400 apiece. She gave me the commission, saying I was batting 1,000 so far…. So, I took some pictures and she sent the originals back.

I explained the process, which would take some time, about a month and that I would have them ready for a big birthday party they were throwing for a movie star friend of theirs. After a month of work, I delivered not only the four, but another six that were similar. She bought them all. Then she had the caretakers and maids fill them with fresh flowers just in time for the festivities.

The designers saw them and asked if I had made these. I told them yes, and I can do it again. They said we should come out with a line and I could make the pottery and they would sell them…like in New York, and Chicago, and that we could make a lot of money with these. I told them that I had schooled with a Dutch Master potter, Sir Weber, and he had taught me all I know.

Mrs. Awesome got word of this and told the designers, "No one else is getting my pottery." So that got scrapped, but I'm still making pots like those to this day.

I kept working on the house as things were added, enjoying every minute. It was the beginning of December, and the Awesomes hired a girl to decorate the house for Christmas. I overheard them talking about three trees and garlands, etc. They told her to pretty much just decorate most of the house and gave her $15,000 to do the job. They wanted it done right away, so she, the Mrs., gave her payment in full so that her crew could start right away and be completely done by the twelfth.

Shortly after the decorator left, the phone rang and

I heard Mrs. Awesome say, "It's the Baron. Join you for Christmas at the castle? How wonderful. We can leave right away." Within an hour the bags were in the limo and the couple was off to Germany to meet the Baron. They didn't come back till after Christmas but called and had the maid take some pictures of all the decorations before they were taken down right after the first of January so they could see what had been done. They'd instructed the caretakers to be sure to turn all the lighting on every night so the neighbors could enjoy!

My final assignment was to decorate the children's playroom. It was quite large with high-pitched ceilings. She wanted me to decorate all the walls, ceiling, and furniture to look like fairyland. The funny thing was that she never asked me what the cost would be. She just said don't get too crazy with the cost.

So, I set about the task of crackling all the furniture in soft white color, with metallic gold background for the cracks. I then hand-painted fairies and swirled the bedposts with flowery vines. Finally, when that was finished, she asked me if I could do anything super with the cabinet doors. So I painted all the insert panels with big rose-y flowers with babies sitting in their centers. By the time it was all done, it was the most fantastic children's playroom ever. I thought this great job was finished, and I would have to go back to doing a health spa or something when she asked, "Can you possibly work at my daughter-in-law's house? They just bought a big brownstone in Bel Air and my designers would like you to be their artist." AWESOME.

DAUGHTER-IN-LAW

I made an appointment to meet with the Awesomes' daughter-in-law, Jean, and their designers. I pulled up to the great big brownstone on about five wooded acres and was set to discuss what they had planned for me to do.

Upon arriving, I parked and went up to the front door. Just then, the head designer came out, sweating, and declared, "I'm being castrated on a daily basis here! Hope you can help us. This woman is impossible." This was a guy who was usually smiling and happy.

I said, "Well, I always carry my invisible bullshit shield and sword of truth. I use these to fend off this type of crap, and when it becomes necessary, I can counter criticisms with a sharp, stabbing remark of my own." He said, "Good luck," and we went in.

At the meeting she and the designers compiled a list of work, and then she quickly disappeared with her girlfriend. I didn't see her again much, just momentarily without any comment from her to me, but I did hear her constantly yelling at the designers. I finished and presented her with the invoice.

She sat down at a desk and began crossing off one thing after another till she had whittled the cost down from $4,200 to $400.

She said, "This is all I'm paying."

"I think you're missing a zero there on the check," but she just got up and walked away.

I was pretty pissed off, but thought about all the good I'd experienced at her mother-in-law's house, so I held my anger in check and said, "Whatever makes you happy." The head designer stopped me and said, "Where's your shield?" I went back to the studio to figure out how to make up for the lost time and revenue.

A couple of weeks later she called me and told me she had some other work for me to do, and asked when I could get it done.

"So let's see, you didn't pay me for the last job and shorted my earnings by $3,800. All you do is yell at people, never happy with anyone's work, and now you ask me to come back and do more work for you. I have a better idea, why don't you go fuck yourself." And then I hung up the phone.

I ended up going back to the Awesomes' house, and was given the job to paint flowers growing out of the baseboards in the children's playroom.

The head designer came over to me and asked what I had said to her and I told him.

"She was nice to us for two days after, but then went back to her regular rants."

"Have to take out the sword!" I said.

THE HAIRDRESSER APT.

I work for insurance companies sometimes and got a call to restore some faux-finished walls at an apartment in Beverly Hills near the design center. I was told that it was for a famous person in the hair and cosmetics industry. We were to meet at his place and decide what could be done to repair the water-damaged walls.

Upon arriving and meeting the insurance people, we went upstairs and entered the apartment after being greeted by the hairstylist's boyfriend. We chatted for a few minutes and he said we needed to wait for his lover. I took this time to review the damage to the walls.

After leaving the room briefly, the boyfriend came back and said he wanted to show me something in the bedroom. I have to say that he was a screaming queen but nonetheless, I accompanied him into the boudoir. After passing larger pictures of some very famous people in the hallway, all autographed with "Love you" and then a signature, we entered the bedroom.

He pointed at a large photograph, say 24" by 36", of a nude male that had been taken from the back or rear view.

He looked at me and said, "This is me! This is me!"

I quickly replied "I thought I recognized you!"

Upon which he slightly screeched and said, "You are such a savage," hugged me and said "Maybe we should get back to the living room" where the insurance people were waiting.

We waited for about an hour for the hairstylist to show. He came in for about two minutes and said he had to get back to his salon and the clients but whatever needed to be done, just do it, and signed the work order. I never did go back to do the work because the insurance people couldn't seem to schedule the work.

GIFT EXCHANGE

I was invited to a Christmas party that was being hosted by the head of a design firm that I had been working with. A gift exchange was planned where each person invited was to bring a gift less than $10, and at a point in the festivities, the packages are exchanged and you are able to keep or trade your gift for someone else's.

Now I knew that at this party there was to be this woman, her name was Maris, say thirty-five-ish in age. She was forever flirting with every man that was around, double-entendres blazing! I mean she never missed an opportunity whether alone or with someone in a group. I thought this an opportune moment to have a little fun, since I drew her name.

I decided to go to Fredrick's of Hollywood and get something racy. I found a pair of red, crotchless panties and had them gift-wrapped, then went over to the party. As I entered the party of maybe fifty people, I set the package down with everyone else's, and began to mingle. As I talked to a couple of people about the white elephant thing, they informed me that it wasn't anonymous, sending a chill up my spine. I quickly went back to the table but the gifts had already been collected.

I began to sweat. I needed a drink! I was just about to leave when I got dragged back into the living room for the gift exchange to begin. After a few packages, they got to mine and handed it to "M" saying it was from David DeMars. Heat is what I was feeling as she peeled off the wrapping and held up the panties. There was silence first, then some laughter, and someone said something under their breath that was hard to make out. "M" blushed deep red and gave me a "look." I grinned, sheepish, and backed out of the crowd. I guess my idea kind of backfired.

VAN NUYS GIRL

I've gotten a little help I don't really need.

I had a big job starting in about a week, so I decided to put out a call for some help. The ad read— "Experienced painter needed for graphics work…only experienced people need apply."

I put the ad in and got several calls right away, but by asking a few pertinent skill-related questions, I was unable to find the right person. Then the phone rang and a girl called and began to tell me that she had been painting for a long time and that she needed the work. After a few questions, though, I realized she didn't have the skills required.

Somehow during the conversation, I mentioned the address of the jobsite and she apparently picked up on that info because she showed up at the job the next day.

She was quite pretty and probably about nineteen or twenty and she approached me after locating me in the hallway where I was starting to paint the graphic designs that were to accent each doorway.

She sort of began to beg me for the work, but I said I was sorry, but she didn't have the skills required. She left but came back after about a half hour with the old gentleman whose project this was. Apparently she had convinced him with her charms, and got him to practically order me that I had to give her the work as a favor to him. I gave in and said okay and the old guy went back to his office on the first floor of the building.

I was a little miffed, but decided I had no choice, so I asked her if she could help me move all the paint down to the end of the hallway. The first thing she did was pick up the two open gallons of paint (no lids) and try to carry them both with one hand, causing paint to start to spill as she started to walk to the other end of the hall. With each step, the paint began to pour out onto the brand-new carpet that had been installed the day before.

I immediately stopped her, took the paint cans from her and put them back on the scaffold where they had been. I simply said, "Oh, great," knowing I had a new task at hand to clean the carpet as quickly as I could, before the paint began to dry. Once dried I'd never get it out and would have to pay for the carpet.

I didn't say anything to her, because I had to act quickly to get the necessary rags and water bucket that I needed. I ran downstairs and got my stuff to return to the scene of the paint spill. She had left. At least that's what I thought. I worked furiously for about forty minutes to soak up and clean the paint from the carpet until I was dripping with sweat.

About the time I had the problem cleaned up, the girl reappeared with her boyfriend carrying a roll of paper towels. She then exclaimed that she had gone down to the office of the owner and told him that I had spilled a lot of paint on the carpet and that she needed some paper towels to clean up the mess.

"Oh great!"

She then explained that the guy with her was her boyfriend and if I needed some more help painting, he was available as well to work.

I looked at both of them and asked if they had eaten lunch yet, and they replied, "No." I said, "That's good, why don't you go have some lunch and figure out what you're going to do with the rest of your day."

Because I really didn't need their kind of help if you know what I mean.

As soon as I said this, they both looked at each other and the girl then asked, "Well, we've been here for an hour, could we get paid?"

At this point, I'll be honest, I didn't know what to say, but I believe when they looked at my expression they got the message and the message was a resounding "NO!" I then proceeded unaided to move the paint down the hallway as I shook my head in disbelief.

When I looked back they had gone, and I promised myself that I wouldn't ask for "help" ever again.

AH MEN

Back at the studio, I got a referral saying I should contact a gentleman who wanted a mural painted in a fine clothing store down on Santa Monica Boulevard and La Cienega in Los Angeles. I met with the two owners and they showed me the concept sketch for the mural that was to go up on the soffit area above the counter where the cash register was.

The drawing was of two men in speedo bathing suits, arms over each other's shoulders and walking down a beach with the sunset behind them. We agreed on a price and I started the next day.

The clothing store was large and nearing the end of construction and was open, though some areas were not finished. The name of the store was "Ah Men" and basically sold to the gay community. The two male owners were a gay couple.... Let me tell you, they had great clothes, very expensive, in this shop, and I bought some at their smaller store across the street.

I set up the scaffold and painted the mural in two

days and was just about to finish when Jeremy, one of the owners approached me.

"Say, David, I was wondering if you could do me a favor?"

"Yeah, what's that?"

"I would like you to put a bigger basket on the man on the left," he said.

Hmmm, a bigger basket? … Basket? … They're not on a picnic … bigger basket? It finally dawned on me what he was thinking.

"Oh, a bigger basket on the speedos. Right?"

"Yes, thank you. I'll come back in a while to take a look."

I thought to have some fun with this so I took the blue color of the speedo and proceeded to paint the speedos so they looked as if they were stuffed with a large cucumber, or possibly a summer squash, so that the bulge was almost to his knees.

Jeremy came back around the corner, and upon seeing, he exclaimed, "OH MY GOD, that's too much!" After a moment of pondering, he gave a look and said, "Somewhat less please."

I put the speedo back so he had a good handful, and got approval to finish. As I was completing the final touches, people were beginning to roam about the store shopping.

In the corner of the dressing area, the walls were

all mirrored. There were a couple of guys trying on underwear and checking out how they looked from the back. At that point, I had to get out of there. I went into the office, was thanked for a great job, got paid, and left.

GOTTA LOVE YOUR WORK

I had to drive over and take a meeting with this woman. She wanted me to marbleize some columns in her entrance and living room. A huge home, the columns were about two feet in diameter and about ten feet high. All the floors were done in a cream-colored marble, so I suggested to her what we could do was bring this color, the cream marble, up into the columns where it would be soft and beautiful and wouldn't take over prominence in the room. I thought this would be the right direction for her. She thought, "Oh that would be fine," but was wondering how much it would cost. I said that usually these columns were done at about $350–400 apiece. She had about ten, so we were looking at $4,000 for this marbleizing project.

But I said, "I think it would be a beautiful thing for your interior if in fact, you would like to do that."

She said, "Well, I tell you, I think that is exactly what I want to do. It would be perfect! I've been waiting so long to have this done. The only thing I have to tell you, is please do not tell my husband how much it costs. Work that out with me and I will tell him something else because I don't want him to know at all how much I'm paying for this."

I said, "Well, usually I don't do that, but if that is what you want I will try to keep my pricing quiet. If he asks me, I'll just say I gave your wife the estimate on a piece of paper and he can take a look at that."

So she hired me and gave me the deposit and I proceeded to take about a week to a week and a half, to paint these marbleized, cream-colored columns. When I was done it looked absolutely fantastic. I'd perfected a technique that I had been using for years and they were a gorgeous addition to the interior. I was finished and was wrapping up, packing my things to leave when I saw that here was coming the husband. She had just paid me the check and then kind of disappeared upstairs.

The husband approached me and said, "Excuse me, sir."

I said, "Yes, sir?"

He said, "Are you the artist who actually did these columns?"

I said, "Yes. I'm just finishing, packing up my gear here. I think they turned out really nice."

He commented, "I want to shake your hand. This is absolutely some of the most fabulous work I've seen! It really did something tremendous for our home. I'm so very proud of it and I want to thank you for doing such a fine job."

I said, "Well, thank you very much. I take a lot of pride in what I do and wanted to do a super job for you. Thank you for the work. If you have anything else for me, give me a call. Here's my card."

He took my card and thanked me again and was looking at the columns. As I turned to go to the door he said, "I just have a question for you…."

I said, "Well, yes, sir, what is that?"

"You know, this is such quality work, I just can't understand how you can make any money doing this for $25 apiece."

All I could say is "If you're an artist, you've gotta love the work."

GAS STATION

I pulled into the filling station and hopped out to put some gas in. It seems these days that whenever I stop for gas, I get approached by someone looking for a handout of some kind.

These days it's almost never 25 cents or 50 cents, instead it's a couple of dollars or someone needs some gas. Now, gas being about $4.25 a gallon, that isn't 25–50 cents. That's money.

On this particular day, as I pulled the nozzle from the pump, a young man came out from around the other side. He proceeded to say, "Hello. How you doin'? Say, I have to go to a job interview and I just need a couple of gallons to get there. If I can get this job, I'll be able to take care of my wife and baby."

I continued to listen to his sad story about how he had been struggling to get by. I noticed, though, he was driving a better car than I.

I still felt some compassion for his plight, so I decided to use my credit card to get him his two gallons, even though that's about $9.00.

I stepped around the other side of the pump, pulled out the nozzle and was about to push the grade selection on the pump at regular 87 test—$3.98 per gallon.

He quickly caught my hand and said, "No, premium!"

I looked at him through squinty eyes, then put the handle and nozzle back into the gas pump.

"Sorry, dude, your gas offer has been revoked!"

I then went on my way, shaking my head in disbelief as he approached another customer.

ORANGE CRUSH

A man, Mr. Smith, called me and said he found my number online in the Yellow Pages. He saw my website and wanted me to come over and paint a mural for him. He was local, so I arranged to see him later that day.

I drove over to his place, turning down the street to see a typical modern housing tract where all the houses are tan, or light goldfish tan, or gray tan… mostly tan with white trim.

When I came to Mr. Smith's house, I stopped abruptly. The reason I stopped was the house had been painted in a strong peach color with intense orange trim. Now, not the whole house, just the entire front. I said to myself, "Interesting."

I knocked on the front door and Mr. Smith greeted me and asked me inside. I figured he was about fifty-five to sixty years old and had just had a lot of coffee, if you know what I mean.

Within thirty seconds of my arrival, Mr. Smith escorted me out to the front of the house and then proceeded to explain where he wanted me to paint. The doors were one large two-car garage door and one, one-car garage door. We went back inside.

He quickly asked, "How much for the mural?"

"Depends on what you would like as an image, of course, but about $2,000 would be fair."

He whipped out his checkbook, wrote the check and handed it to me saying, "Could you get this done right away?"

"What about the content of the mural? What do you want?"

He said, "Whatever you think."

"How about a desert landscape?"

"Okay," he said.

I said I could start tomorrow, giving me enough time to gather the proper materials. "I'll see you tomorrow then."

"We will be out of town for a few days. How long will it take, two to three days? You can paint it while we're gone."

"That sounds about right. I'll see you when you return." The whole meeting took less than fifteen minutes.

The next day I went to the house, wondering what I could possibly paint that wouldn't look like hell. I figured I could somehow incorporate the orange and tan colors, those that you can see in a desert sunset.

The drop cloths were spread out and the edges were all taped and paper wrapped as I set it up to start to paint the mural. Landscapes are typically easy for me. Sky, ground, and foliage.

I had been painting for about an hour and a half when I suddenly heard a loud voice shout, "Oh no, what's that crazy asshole doing to his house now!" This guy then proceeded to go on yelling and yelling and yelling until I finally turned to take a look.

The guy was a real big biker, complete with a lot of tattoos, black beard, and leathered clothes. Behind him was his friend or roommate whose whole neck and part of his face was covered with tattoos, and a bandana wrapped around his head.

I resumed painting as he quieted down for a moment, but then he revved up his bellowing, and I found it impossible to paint under these circumstances.

I put my brushes in water, covered the paint palette with plastic quickly and started to walk over to the house on the corner where the guy was yelling.

The two saw me coming over. They stopped yelling and went into the house. Their garage door was open and I stopped at the edge to shout, "Hello… Hello…."

The two came out and gave me a dirty look. However, I don't intimidate easily.

"Hello, I'm the artist that was hired to paint this mural over at your neighbor's house. if you don't mind, I'd like to just finish the mural so I can get paid and be able to buy food and such, you know, like rent…. As soon as I'm finished and gone, you can do anything you want, just wait 'til I'm done. Thanks."

They both looked at each other, shrugged their shoulders and went back inside.

I worked the rest of the day and luckily when I came back to finish the next day, the mural hadn't been vandalized. I finished the mural and packed up to go. Looking back at the house as I drove away I thought, "I'll give it two weeks…."

CRAIGSLIST FILM PRODUCER

I responded to a Craigslist ad for an artist. The job description was to paint on a pinball machine and the artist must have "very good painting skills." I got a response within a few moments.

The ad placer said he saw my website and would like to meet so he could show me the project he had in mind. I agreed to meet with him the next day at a house in the Hollywood Hills. He said to bring some paintings he saw on my website as he might be interested in buying a piece or two, but he would have to see "the real thing" to decide.

I arrived on time at a gate that was locked, to a driveway that seemed to wind around the side of the mountain to a home nestled there on the side of the hill in a canyon paralleled to Laurel Canyon in the Hollywood Hills. There was no one around, but I decided to wait.

Soon enough, a car pulled up behind me and the driver got out to open the gate, stopped at my window and asked if I was the artist who was to meet and do the pinball machine painting. I said yes, and he opened the gate and we both drove down the driveway to the house.

The house was a five-bedroom home, built in the late '40s style, with a view of the canyon and an infinity pool in the back, that overlooked the canyon.

We both got out of our vehicles and I went over to meet the man and introduce myself. He asked me to bring in whatever artwork I had brought so he could see it, and then he would show me what he wanted to do with the pinball machine. He was very anxious.

There were boxes and furnishings scattered about. He had just bought the house and was planning on moving in soon. While he and his assistant roamed about the house, I brought in twenty paintings and then placed them around the living room just beyond the entrance.

He and his assistant looked at the works and commented how they loved everything, then asked me to go into the kitchen to look at the pinball project that he had in mind.

The pinball machine was a playboy version, complete with Hugh Hefner next to several playboy models. What his idea was, was to put his new girlfriend's face to replace one of the models on the glass picture at the back of the machine. He commented that his girlfriend had bigger tits. He gave me a picture of her, and instructed me to replace the middle girl's face, with the face of his girlfriend. He seemed a little bit drunk and in the time he explained I took the pictures and the backplate from the machine and agreed on a $350 price to do the portrait of his girlfriend on the glass.

We went back into the living room where the paintings were and discussed which, if any, of the pieces he may be interested in buying.

He said he liked everything but wanted to make a decision after looking at them for a while and he would tell me what he wanted on my return with the glass portrait pinball job.

We agreed on a $1,000 deposit and he wrote me a check. I took the playboy glass plate and the pictures of his girlfriend and put them into the van and told him I'd email him as soon as it was ready. This guy sounded kind of crazy, though.

About a week later, having completed all the preliminary work-ups, I emailed him stating that his work was ready and that I would like to deliver, and talk about the art he perhaps wanted for his home. The email was short, but I thought that perhaps I was going to get manipulated about the paintings, so I commented in the email how artists are typically not paid very well for their work.

At 6:00 a.m. the next morning, I answered the

phone to hear this guy screaming obscenities to ??? of who did I think I am! "You fucking Craigslist asshole. I ???? to ???? this shit and it's ruined my whole day. You can come and pick up your fucking paintings and give me my $1,000 back." He went on with his cursing.

I said that would be fine, and he said to talk with his assistant to arrange a time to pick up the paintings. You see, $1,000 for twenty paintings is about $50 apiece, and I figured this guy was so off the wall that he might think that the $1,000 was for all twenty pieces. He cleared that up by cussing a blue streak, which assured me that he wasn't interested in paying anything close to real value. The phone call ended by me saying that I would contact his assistant to pick up the work, which I did that day, and arranged to recover the paintings the next day.

I arrived with my girlfriend to meet his assistant and load up the work. Since the producer was such an asshole, I delivered the playboy pinball glass and pictures without any work being done, as I chose to put it back to its original condition and he could find somebody else to do his bidding.

I gave his assistant the pinball stuff and began loading the van with my girlfriend, carefully stacking the work and being quiet about it. I didn't need any more drama.

At one point, my girlfriend loaded two Picasso lithographs that were pencil signed into the van… thinking they were mine.

"No, sweetheart, those are Picassos!" I put them back in the house, though I was very tempted to keep them because he was such a dick.

We finished loading and as I shook the assistant's hand, he commented, "Yeah, I know he's an asshole, but I'm trying to cultivate a relationship with him so I can get a room in the house."

Birds of a feather, as they say.

MARVIN GARDENS

Work was slow, so I decided to look in the want ads for some possible employment and found an ad that read "Art Gallery Assistant needed…good pay." I thought this might be a good opportunity for me so I gave the phone number on the ad a call to see if the position had been filled.

A man answered and asked me about my qualifications and education in the art field, and then he agreed to meet me for an interview.

He gave me the name of a place on La Cienega in the center of the art district called "Marvin Gardens," then followed with the address.

He asked me how he could recognize me when I arrived, and asked for a description of me so that we could meet easily. I told him I was about 6' tall, blond hair, slim, and would be wearing a black turtleneck sweater. I then asked how I could recognize him. He replied, "I have big brown eyes." For some reason, this didn't register properly for me.

I went down to the place to meet and brought my

portfolio, arriving a little early so as not to make anyone wait. There was an exterior patio in front and I took a seat at one of the tables, and began to look around.

After about ten minutes, I noticed that there were a lot of men, but no women, and I started thinking about the "big brown eyes" statement and began to feel a little uncomfortable. I decided to go inside to see if I should still interview, 'cause I'm a dumbass and the real situation I was in hadn't registered.

As I went in, it fully registered, believe me. The place was full to capacity, complete with two guys in G-strings dancing on the bar. Loud music playing and I suddenly felt all eyes were on me. One of the dancers stopped for a second, pointed at me and said, "I'll take six of those!"

I looked around and moved quickly to the back of the place where a phone was and the back door. I was back in my van before you could say "Eric Robinson" and took off back to the studio. This wasn't the job for me.

RESTORATION

I landed a job doing the restoration of the historic buildings in Santa Barbara, California. My job was to repaint in exactly the same colors and designs that had been done in 1902.

Originally the paint was done mixing berries and different forms of oxide materials mixed with oil to produce a paint-like substance. The suggested material to repaint was a modern acrylic medium and would be applied after sealing the existing colors because the original paint had chalked out and become very powdery to the touch, as well as very faded. The projected completion of this project was a ninety-day window and the Pearl Clams Society, who raised the money had already planned and established an unveiling before I even began…No pressure there.

The contracts were signed and I began the work, which was all mapped out by the city architect and each color and design was to match his diagrams that he must have spent a lot of time on. Luckily for me, he was not anal.

I set up a scissor lift that had to be on top of a plywood base so that the wheels didn't disturb or scar the old stone floor that was underneath the ceiling that was to be redone.

Each day I would start at 8:00 a.m., go up to the ceiling about sixty feet up and attach color samples to be okayed by the architect whom I saw on a pretty much daily basis.

All of these designs were of family crests that were prominent in the town in 1902.

This ceiling was part of the courthouse, where the business of jurisprudence transpired far below the scaffold and I observed many people going to and leaving the courthouse, some happy and some in tears.

The grand jury room was on the same level as my scaffold and I was forced to hear the chatter this committee-like group dictating out the fates of many a poor soul.

I pressed on day after day, while spending the nights by the beach. Though this may sound interesting, it was a particularly tough gig, but eventually I completed the project down to the day that it was to be for the banquet for the society people.

It was at this point that they told me that I was not invited to the unveiling. This was total bullshit and I let them know how I felt. Apparently they decided to invite me then.

I attended the dinner, but they never mentioned my name, as the architect and his assistant took complete credit for this accomplishment. Nice, huh? I did, however, get a full-page spread in the local newspaper, titled "ARCH ANGEL" since the ceiling was a huge arch-shaped ceiling. On to the next I guess.

I was checking into one of the hotels there, and saw an old painting 6' X 8' I had done many years back hanging behind the desk. A large abstract with the word "Hotel" painted atop a lot of squares and rectangles in various colors. I had originally sold that painting to a doctor who had passed away, and the owner of the hotel had bought it from the estate sale. I remember when the doctor bought the painting, because he said he liked the painting but wanted me to just change the colors…hello…I assured him that it wouldn't be the same painting, and so he decided to buy it as it was. Art that is purchased and sold, begins a life of its own.

Towards the end of finishing the ceiling, a production film crew came into town to shoot a film called It's Complicated with Meryl Streep, Steve Martin, and Alex Baldwin. They shut down the streets adjacent to the courthouse and set up a flea market for a big shot for the film. There were about a hundred people on the crew, as well as a tremendous amount of equipment. The city officials were angry because they were saying that the Hollywood people were taking over. Since where I was painting would be in the background, I was wondering if I might see myself in the film. After six days of shooting, and I would assume a lot of money spent, they wrapped up the set and began to break it down. I got down off the scaffold, went over to the set and the production crew gave me all the flowers and strawberries and such, or they said they would just be thrown out.

When I went to see the film, this portion of the film maybe lasted ten seconds. That's a lot of coin for ten seconds, I figure.

Oh well, back to the salt mines.

SMILEY'S

Woke up and started to listen to a little Carlos Jobim on the record player cause they had record players at the time. And it was all mellow but then the phone rang. I had to go out of town for my next job. I had to fly in a plane up to Beaverton, Oregon and decorate for a guy we'll call Mr. M. Everybody was afraid of him. He had a lot of money and was quite eccentric.

I flew into town. Before I could start the job he asked me to come up to his chateau because he had a little problem that he wanted me to touch up before I started the murals at his jobsite. I had to get a rent-a-car, so I rented one, got in the car, and drove up to his place on top of the mountain. It was a lot like a castle. I was greeted at the door by the butler. I told him that I was David Paul DeMars, the artist.

He said, "Oh yes. Mr. M. is waiting for you."

I walked down a large, two-door, wooden, coffered castle, into a library area, through the library into a kitchen, through the passageway, and down to where he was in a large hall. The butler said, "Just go through those doors. He is waiting for you."

When I passed through the doors, I went down what seemed like a little bit farther and there was a giant table that probably could have seated about fifty people at something like a large formal dinner with kings and queens. And there, at the end of the table sat my employer, Mr. M., dressed in a SS uniform. His hat was on the table…along with his Luger. Which is, I think a .435 caliber automatic German handgun. And he was quite drunk. I remember he was kinda drunk most of the time that I was working for him. But I liked him. He was pretty cool…till I saw him in his SS uniform. I took him a little more seriously after that.

What he wanted me to do was repair the bullet holes. See, he'd gotten excited and discharged his weapon, hence the bullet holes throughout the room. I had to go out and get some materials to fix that, but I decided I might not want to make a sudden entrance. After fixing everything, I did make a quick exit, then hurried back to the jobsite.

Once I got back to the jobsite, I got set up but then decided to go back to my hotel room. I'd been on the road before and you know, the road was kind of a drag. Why? Well you're in a…town, say like Beaverton, Oregon. There's a whole lot going on there. Unh-hnnh! But then again, no. I'm alone. I sat in the motel room thinking, sitting there at that little table, elbows on the table, slumping, wondering and peering out the window. Contemplating possibly the picture of something else. It had been a long day that day…being out of town in this little hotel room wasn't exactly my idea of a good time. I'd been doing this for quite a while and all you'd do is work…go back to the hotel…watch TV…get up…work—over and over again.

So I decided…well, that night, Wednesday, I'd go downtown a little bit and check out some of the local haunts even though I was in Beaverton, Oregon. I'd see if I could find myself a little quiet restaurant, maybe sit down and drink a beer. Maybe watch the locals do their thing. You know, I was a little bored with sitting in a hotel room. When you think bored, you're thinking well, it's just the same ole thing over and over again, and you know, maybe something interesting will happen. You never know.

So I said to myself maybe I should go see what the other half was doing. See, you know, if maybe there was a little fun out there. So I decided to go out. So I got up, got the key to the rental car, put on my coat, went outside, and found the rental car the company had provided for me, and I went down until I found a place called "Smiley's."

Smiley's, now that sounds like a friendly place. I

think I'll go in there and see what's happening at Smiley's. Go in, have a beer, relax a little bit. Shoot pool. I don't know what they got in there. Maybe this would be good for me, so I pulled in the parking lot, parked the car making sure that I had my wallet, keys and all that stuff. I locked the car and went in the front door.

I'd never been in a place quite like this before. There was something about the front door…it was a little different. There was like a ramp going in and a ramp going out. I don't now…a bunch of pool tables. But I thought, well, it's better than being back in that room. It might be a fun place anyways…a couple of moose heads on the walls, dartboards…things like that. And there was a lot of people, a bustling business. I looked down at the sawdust floor, walked over to a booth and sat down. I put on my Harley-Davidson hat—a baseball cap type hat—and decided that, you know, this could be fun. Maybe someone would talk to me about motorcycles. So I settled into this spot.

Sure enough the waitress wandered up and offered me something to drink.

I said, "Sure, I'll have a cold one, whatever you've got on tap."

She said, "Fine," and away she went.

As she walked away I looked around and things

seemed to be a little bit different in this restaurant from what I was used to. There was something about the clientele in this establishment that seemed a little strange. For one thing, there was a big guy, kind of draped over this pool table. He was about 250 pounds, with a large tattoo on his arm of a skull and flames and he had a mean look in his eye. I'm thinking unh, let's see, maybe I'll just get this beer and get out of here.

After I accepted the beer, I realized, you know, maybe Smiley's wasn't the finest establishment I'd ever been in. In fact it might be described as the worst. I didn't exactly feel like I fit in. In fact, it was a little scary in there.

But there was a thin girl whose hair looked as if it had been in a windstorm smoking a cigarette over to my left. She had a chain collar around her neck, high over-the-knee black boots, and enough makeup for the Rockettes on her face. And the smoke from the cigarette was kind of puffing around her head. I thought "My, what a lovely child."

I had another sip of beer. I was kind of halfway through the beer when the girl walked up and said, "Hey, gee…Harley-Davidson, hunh? I'm into motorcycles. You got a Harley-Davidson?"

I didn't really want to seem like I didn't have a Harley-Davidson so I said, "Yes" and for some reason proceeded to describe how I like riding around carefree as you may be on a Harley-Davidson, even though I didn't really have one, just the hat.

Well, she went on about her stories as she puffed away on her cigarette and teased her hair and her nylons. She went on about all her experiences on a motorcycle…they were pretty colorful let me tell you. But it was interesting! Even though she didn't seem real educated, it was kind of fascinating.

She said, "I'd like a beer. How about if you buy me a beer?"

I said, "Well, I'm just gonna finish this one and then get out of here, but it was nice chatting with you."

About this time a 300 pound…large woman, scooted in and sort of knocked me over to the side of the booth, hemming me in so I couldn't get out. Now, I wouldn't call her petite. I'm talking about 300 pounds and unbathed.

The big girl started giggling and playing with her friend…apparently the girl who had sat down first was her friend. They started chattering about this and chattering about that, and I couldn't figure out how to get out of there. I was almost out of beer and I was only planning to have that one but now I had this giant woman next to me. I thought to myself, I gotta leave. Like now. At about that point, the girl who'd first sat down across the table from me said, "Hey, you wanna see something?"

I said, "Like what?"

"I'd like to show you my tattoo."

She leaned over and pulled out her breast and exposed a dragon that was circling her entire titty with the head resting upon her nipple. Around and around it went until it ended up somewhere about her shoulder. Well…that was quite a tattoo. But I'm starting to wonder about my future…immediate future.

She kinda said, "Hey, ain't that pretty neat hunh?"

Yeah! And then she kept on talking with the big woman who had trapped me in the booth. I was starting to panic at this point cause I was out of beer, and I was trapped by a big, fat, stinky woman and the girl I now refer to as Dragon Tit. At that point I also happened to notice, cause I'd been in there for an entire beer, that the rest of the clientele of Smiley's was some of the most low-down looking cutthroats that I'd ever had the misfortune to cross paths with.

Frankly, I had to get out of that place. But it was kind of hard because I was trying to keep my composure at the same time, I had to get out! My hotel room was not looking too bad at this point.

However, the big mama to my left had me penned in the booth. And now I had a 6'8" black individual with a pretty gnarly scar on his right cheek. It went through part of his mouth and his eye.

"You know, Big Leroy ain't gonna like you talkin' with nobody else."

The girl across the table says, "I know, I know, I'm not real worried about it. Besides he's not even here."

Well, at this point, the door kind of opened, you know that front door that I'd come through, and in walked a fairly burly-looking individual. Had hair kinda past his shoulders, straight and black. He had a black beard and a jean vest, frayed around the sleeves, chain hangin' from the belt, large motorcycle boots, somewhat greasy motorcycle pants, yelling, "Big Leroy's pulling in here. He's going to flip his bike around and slide it up and park it next to the curb!"

Now, the whole crowd kinda ran around to the front door and looked outside. So I stood up. The exit was blocked and there was no back door. Here I saw this motorcycle speeding right for the place, right for the front door. Suddenly he slammed on the brakes and the bike slid around and caused this huge dust cloud. Apparently what Big Leroy was trying to do was park this thing cool, but he didn't quite make it.

What happened was he hit this piece of concrete. He and the bike flew up in the air with him and the motorcycle landing in a bush way off to the side. There was a hush over the crowd. But here the next thing I see is Big Leroy climbing out of the bush telling everybody to get outa his way cause he's gotta pull his bike out of the bush. He got it straightened out and started it up. Everybody started laughing.

Now, I'm still trapped inside. The girl turns to me and says, "I can't wait for you to meet Leroy. He's a real piece of work."

She starts pushing me back to the booth. I'm shaking in my boots. The girl asks me if I could loan her $40.00. She'd pay me back cause she saw it in my wallet and she could sure use it and she'd appreciate it and she'd give me her address and so on and so forth.

"Well, I'm sorry, but I gotta go! I think I should get some work done back at the hotel."

She said, "I could really use the money. Please loan it to me."

I kinda said, "No." But as I started to get out of the booth again she grabbed my arm and said, "Come on, help me out."

When I pulled my arm away, she slipped, fell down and hit her head. Next thing I knew, there's a guy in the corner saying, "Hey! Somebody hurt Big Leroy's girlfriend!"

I took off running out of there!

GOD'S DOOR

It wasn't long after I had finished a rather long and difficult assignment, when I got an offer from a designer to do some murals at a complex next to the Academy of Science and Industry building in North Hollywood California.

After some preliminary meetings, the murals were to depict television stars' portraits done like a graphite drawing in gray tones. The committee chose about forty stars, and the sites for the illustrations to go in transitional corridors that were lighted by large windows. I made an excellent deal with the committee and began the work the following week.

I set up in one area, and began the work when I smelled pretty toxic fumes coming down the hallway where I had started. So, I went to see what was going on to find the painting crew was still spraying lacquer cabinets in all the units on that floor. They informed me that they were a bit behind schedule, and that they would be doing this spraying throughout the complex to make sure they made the deadline commitment to the general contractor.

I was on a strict schedule myself, so I had to get back to my work to keep up with the demands on the deadline schedule.

These murals were fairly simple illustrations that were done by using the provided pictures of the stars projected on the wall one at a time to create groups of five or six portraits. I used an art brush and gray acrylic paint done like a watercolor, and the paintings went up quite quickly, so I moved down the hall past where the painters were spraying the lacquer, and this went on all week until Friday when it was time to knock of and regroup on Monday. Upon arriving back at the studio, I noticed I felt very ill.

I began to feel dizzy and had a hard time breathing. That's when I realized I had been breathing lacquer fumes all week. I decided to go to the ER to get some diagnosis and remedy for the symptoms I was experiencing. As I drove it seemed that I was feeling worse by the minute.

When I arrived at the ER, I was taken in and the doctor. A young black man, said he needed some X-rays taken of my chest after I told him what had transpired on the jobsite and the lacquer fumes that were present there.

He came back with some bad news. He informed me that the lacquer fumes had coated the inside of my lungs and that I needed some heavy antibiotics to stave of the infection. He gave me a shot and handed me a bottle of pills and said, I think you'll make it" and pointed to an elderly woman across from me and then said, "She's not going to make it." He told me to go home and rest and that I still looked strong.

I went back to the studio and lay down and went to sleep. The next morning I felt much worse and had a high temp, that stayed with me for the next five days. Like 105. The fifth day I could hardly breathe and my body was working hard to somehow supply me with enough oxygen. I felt like I was running in a never-ending marathon.

That's when I thought I was going to die, and I was going to give up, when I noticed a small white dot on the ceiling over my head. The dot grew until the whole room was all white and I began to hear celestial sounds. These were accompanied by about a million gold and silver angels transcending upward into infinity. I no longer felt any pain whatsoever, and it seemed I was being invited to join. I was about to give it up, when a child's face appeared and seemed to tell me not to go, because I was needed here on earth.

The next thing I realized upon waking up, was that the fever had broken and I was feeling better although quite exhausted.

I waited another day to recuperate before going back to the jobsite to complete the murals. When I ran into the superintendent in charge of the project and he asked where I had been. I told him I got ill and that "I lived."

He said, "Well, get back to work, we're on a DEADLINE."

DRUNKEN GLITTER PAINTINGS

I had a party for some friends at the studio, and some friends of friends. There was lots of loud music, alcohol, and a little weed got passed around.

Things were rolling along when I suggested that everyone go out in the back for a "conceptual art experience." I had laid out a bunch of canvases on the ground and had dozens of cups filled with colors of paint. Each person was allowed to take three cups to toss at the canvases from behind a line that was ten feet away. It started out fine, but soon got out of control when I introduced the glitter packages I had left over from painting a set for a film I'd worked on. Paint was flying. Glitter was being sprinkled like fairy dust until all was used up. Then everyone went back inside, and continued to party till the night was through.

The next morning, I went out and gathered up the canvases and stacked them in a corner of the studio, wondering what I would do with these.

Sometime later someone referred a gallery owner to come and see my work. She arrived at the studio, driving a Mercedes and looking quite dolled up. We talked for a while and she pondered over some of the paintings I had done, she then found the stacked glitter paintings in the corner. Of all my work, she chose THOSE!

She wanted me to deliver them to her gallery on La Cienega in the arts district of Beverly Hills, and we would install them. There were fourteen in all, ranging from 2x3 feet to 4x5 feet and filled the walls of her gallery with the canvases. She had taken them on consignment and she attached fairly large price tags on them. She said she was going out of town, and she sent me a check for the entire amount a few days later after she found out that I already had a girl friend.

ART EXPERIENCE

Since the last paintings were such a success, I decided to have some friends over for a conceptual art experience—making an abstract painting. The studio was on a big property so I built a small wall out of wood on which I would hang a big canvas and I would suspend a lot of spray paint cans from string from this bar in front of the canvas.

The party game would be to stand back, probably… oh fifty feet, and we would shoot the cans with a .22 rifle thereby puncturing the cans. The cans would spray around and make all these spray marks on the canvas.

I thought by the time the party was over there would be bullet holes, possibly spray paint marks, and maybe a little glitter at the end. Everybody would have a kick out of the fun, and eventually, at the end of the party there would be a way-out abstract painting.

That night everybody came over, about ten folks. We partied and had some drinks. The girls couldn't wait to shoot this .22 at the spray paint cans.

Everybody was getting excited. All the music got cranked up, the party was rolling along but pretty soon it started to get dark. Everyone came out to do the conceptual art experience painting. It was a little too dark to see well but someone came up with the idea to light some candles and put them on the table in front of the paintings so we could see the canvas as we shot the spray paint cans with the .22.

We got some candles…set them up…and lit them. I got to take the first shot but when I fired the first shot, I missed…. Everybody said, "Wow!"

I hit the can with the second shot but because of the candles, the spray paint can exploded and a fireball about 25 feet in diameter blew out from that can. It looked like the birth of a star. Everybody was standing with their mouths open in awe. If it had been a little closer there would have been a lot of charred faces. It came almost up to us and stopped, and then we all looked back at the canvas and it was on fire.

We all stood there and watched the canvas burn. The canvas burned pretty quick, except for the wood stretcher bars. I ran back inside and hid the gun. Everybody thought it was a really great conceptual art experience because no one got hurt. We went back inside and kept partying.

THE DREAM GIRL

I had grown tired of the nights out roaming the city, the clubs…it seemed as though the endless stream of dates and encounters with girls never amounted to more than something like unfinished business. It's not that I wasn't enjoying myself. It just seemed as though something was missing…as if a great puzzle had been laid out, but there were some pieces missing.

It was then that a friend gave me the phone number of a girl that she knew from ballet class that she said I might have something in common with. She gave me the number on a scratch piece of paper and I put it in my wallet thinking maybe I would call the girl later if I felt like it.

Later that evening I was restless as usual, so I decided to call.

The girl answered and we chatted for a little while and arranged a meeting at her mother's house, where she was staying at the time. The days before the meeting went as usual, whatever usual was…

typically the unusual, as that had been my regular pattern. Nothing was ever boring.

It was a Friday night and I drove the van to her home only a few miles away. I parked and went to the door of a charming old house, well-wooded and landscaped with fruit trees and flowers. I reached the door and just as I was about to ring the bell, the door opened. The most beautiful girl I had ever seen opened the door and the only thing I could think of to say was "Ding dong." She giggled and smiled and invited me in where I met her mother and we sat chatting over tea and cheesecake. I remember as she excused herself to leave the room, she looked back just before the hallway opening and glanced at me and kicked up one of her legs and smiled in a whimsical dance. I was smitten.

We chatted for a little longer and I said I ought to leave and that perhaps we could see each other again. I would call her on the morrow to arrange a date. I guess she had wanted to meet me on her turf where she felt safe because a guy who needed to get a girl's number from a friend might be some kind of creep.

I called and asked her out to dinner and she said yes, so I decided on a place I knew called The Aware Inn. It was a nice bistro that served salads and such as I remembered she'd said she was a vegetarian and on a strict diet because she was a professional dancer with extensive training in the art.

On the way to dinner, I decided to tell her that I wanted to give her a kiss and get the anxiety of the end-of-the-date-kiss over with early. We kissed…and the chemistry of that kiss I will never forget.

Over dinner we chatted about our lives, how we came to be where we were, and the more I got to know her, the more of her I wanted to know. She was deep and intelligent as well as beautiful and I wondered if I had a chance at capturing her heart for however long I might be able to keep her interested in me. I thought that I would enjoy her company for as long as I could, never thinking that me, an artist with no money or station in life, could possibly keep her interested for very long.

I took her home and kissed her again at the door and she kissed me in return. I thought then that maybe I had a chance with her. I told her that I would call her tomorrow and we could talk and maybe arrange to see each other again.

The next day I called, dismissing the three-day rule which I personally thought was ridiculous. We saw each other again and went to the beach at night and talked and languished the night away. She was so wonderful. I took her home and asked to see her again soon, as I couldn't get enough of her.

I invited her to my place for a quick dinner and to listen to some music by the fireplace. After dinner, in front of the fire, the real blaze began and this blaze continued for many days and nights thereafter. We had become lovers and I had fallen madly for her, still thinking that I would enjoy her for as long as I could. This went on for weeks.

She became my world. I would sit with her and she would read aloud while I painted painting after painting with her by my side.

One night, after weeks of loving her, I found myself so enraptured with her as we made love, like a trance or a spell that I was under, that I asked her to marry me. Not on one knee, but on elbows and knees. She said yes.

We then planned the wedding with a few friends in a small chapel and as I saw her coming down the aisle, I knew that this long search was over and that I was a very lucky fellow.

It wasn't long after the wedding and honeymoon in Hawaii that we moved into a small rental house. She soon got news of a job in a musical play and that she was offered a great part as a principal dancer. We would need to make ready to leave town and reestablish ourselves in San Francisco where the play was being produced at the Orpheum Theatre.

We moved into a small apartment just off the

cable-car route, where we could take the cable car to and from the theatre each evening for the performance, then back to the apartment at the end of the show to love each other to death each night.

It wasn't long before the costumer said that her costume wasn't fitting properly and informed her that perhaps she was pregnant. As it turns out, she was. She finished the play after several months and we returned to start our new lives as parents.

But that's another story.

To this day, I would gladly give up my life for her, as she is a better person than I. I always thought, from the moment that I met her, that she was going to change my life for the better, and she did.